ISBN 978-1-330-18040-2
PIBN 10046040

Forgotten Books is a registered trademark of FB &c Ltd.
Copyright © 2018 FB &c Ltd.
FB &c Ltd, Dalton House, 60 Windsor Avenue, London, SW19 2RR.
Company number 08720141. Registered in England and Wales.

For support please visit www.forgottenbooks.com

1 MONTH OF
FREE
READING

at

www.ForgottenBooks.com

By purchasing this book you are eligible for one month membership to ForgottenBooks.com, giving you unlimited access to our entire collection of over 1,000,000 titles via our web site and mobile apps.

To claim your free month visit:

www.forgottenbooks.com/free46040

English
Français
Deutsche
Italiano
Español
Português

www.forgottenbooks.com

Mythology Photography **Fiction**
Fishing Christianity **Art** Cooking
Essays Buddhism Freemasonry
Medicine **Biology** Music **Ancient**
Egypt Evolution Carpentry Physics
Dance Geology **Mathematics** Fitness
Shakespeare **Folklore** Yoga Marketing
Confidence Immortality Biographies
Poetry **Psychology** Witchcraft
Electronics Chemistry History **Law**
Accounting **Philosophy** Anthropology
Alchemy Drama Quantum Mechanics
Atheism Sexual Health **Ancient History**
Entrepreneurship Languages Sport
Paleontology Needlework Islam
Metaphysics Investment Archaeology
Parenting Statistics Criminology
Motivational

THE GOLDEN HELM

AND OTHER VERSE

THE
GOLDEN HELM

AND OTHER VERSE

BY

WILFRID WILSON GIBSON

LONDON
ELKIN MATHEWS, VIGO STREET

1903

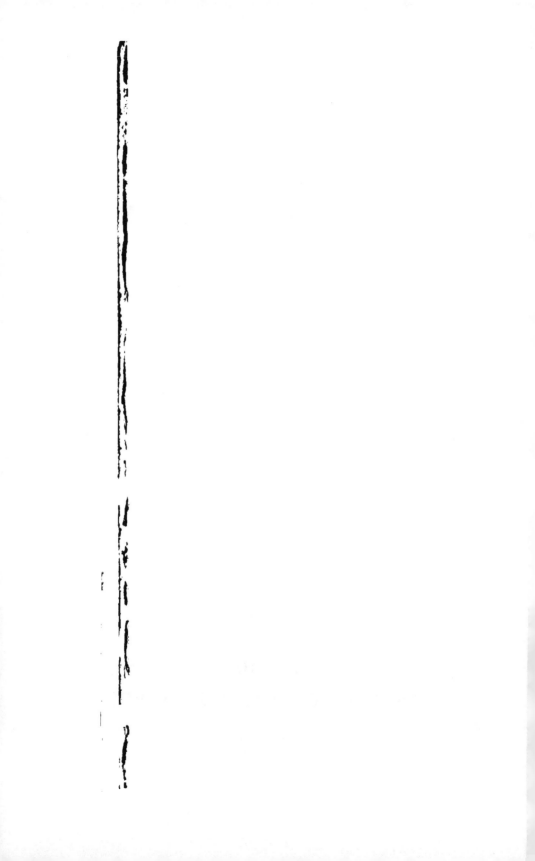

TO

HOWARD PEASE

THANKS are due to Messrs. Smith, Elder, & Co., for permission to reprint "The King's Death," "The Three Kings," and the first part of "Averlaine and Arkeld," from *The Cornhill Magazine*; to the editor of *Macmillan's Magazine* for leave to reprint "In the Valley"; to the editor of *The Saturday Review* for leave to reprint "Notre Dame de la Belle-Verrière"; and to the editors of *The Pilot, The Outlook, The Pall Mall Gazette, Country Life, The Week's Survey,* and *The Broadsheet,* for like courtesy with regard to a number of "The Songs of Queen Averlaine."

Contents

The Torch

THROUGH skies blown clear by storm, o'er
    storm-spent seas,
Day kindled pale with promise of full noon
Of blue unclouded; no night-weary wind
Ruffled the slumberous, heaving deeps to white,
Though round the Farne Isles the waves never
    sink
In foamless sleep—about the pillared crags
For ever circling with unresting spray.
At dawn's first glimmer, from his island-cell—
Rock-hewn, secure from tempest—Oswald came
With slow and weary step, white-faced and worn
With night-long vigil for storm-perilled souls.
His anxious eye with sharp foreboding bright—
He scanned the treacherous flood; the long
    froth-trail
That marks the lurking reefs; the jag-toothed
    chasms

Which, foaming, gape at night beneath the
    keel—
The mouth of hell to storm-bewildered ships:
But no scar-stranded vessel met his glance.
Relieved, he drank the glistering calm of morn,
With nostril keen and warm lips parted wide;
While, gradually, the sun-enkindled air
Quickened his pallid cheek with youthful flame,
Though lonely years had silvered his dark head,
And round his eyes had woven shadow-meshes.
Clearly he caught the ever-clamorous cries
Of guillemot and puffin from afar,
Where, canopied by hovering, white wings,
They crowded naked pinnacles of rock.
He watched, with eyes of glistening tenderness,
The brooding eider—Cuthbert's sacred bird,
That bears among the isles his saintly name—
Breast the calm waves; a black, wet-gleaming
    fin
Cleft the blue waters with a foaming jag,
Where, close behind the restless herring-herd,
With ravening maw of death, the porpoise sped.
Oswald, light-tranced, dreamed in the sun
    awhile;

Till, suddenly, as some old sorrow starts,
Though years have glided by with soothing lull,
The gust of ancient longing rent his bliss:
His narrow isle, as by some darkling spell,
More narrow shrank; the gulls' unceasing cries
Grew still more fretful; and his hermit-life
A sea-scourged desolation to him seemed.
The holy tree of peace—which he had dreamt
Would flourish in the wilderness afresh,
Upspringing ever in new ecstasy
Of branching beauty and white blooms of truth,
Till its star-tangling crest should cleave the sky,
And angels rustle through its topmost boughs—
Seemed sapless, rootless. Through his quiver-
    ing limbs
His famine-wasted youth to life upleapt
With passionate yearning for humanity:
The stir of towns; the jostling of glad throngs;
Welcoming faces and warm-clasping hands;
Yea, even for the lips and eyes of Love
He hungered with keen pangs of old desire:
And, if for him these might not be, he craved
At least the exultation of swift peril—
The red-foamed riot of delirious strife

That rears a bloody crest o'er peaceful shires,
And, slaying, in a swirl of slaughter dies.
With brow uplifted and strained, pulsing throat,
And salt-parched lips out-thrust, unto the sun
He stretched beseeching hands, as though he
      sought
To snatch some glittering disaster thence.
One moment radiant thus ; and then once more
His arms dropped listless, and he slowly shrank
Within his sea-stained habit, cowering dark
Amid the azure blaze of sea and sky.
Then, stirring, with impatient step he moved
Across the isle to where the rocky shore,
Forming a little, crag-encircled bay,
Sloped steeply to the level of the sea ;
But, as he neared the edges of the tide,
Startled, he paused, as, marvelling, he saw
A woman on the shelving, wet, black rock,
Lying, forlorn, among the storm-wrack, white
And motionless ; still wet, her raiment clung
About her limbs, and with her wet, gold hair
Green sea-weed tangled. Oswald on her looked
Amazed, as one who, in a sea-born trance,
Discovers the lone spirit of the storm,

Self-spent at last, and sunk in dreamless
⸢ slumber
Within some caverned gloom. Coldly he
watched
The little waves creep up the glistening rock,
And, faltering, slide once more into the deep,
As though they feared to waken her : at length,
When one, more venturous, about her stole,
And moved her heavy hair as if with life,
He shuddered; and a lightning-knowledge struck
His heart with fear ; and in a flash he knew
That no sea-phantom couched before him lay,
But some frail fellow-creature, tempest-tost,
Hung yet in peril on the edge of death,
Her weak life slipping from the saving grasp
While he delayed. He sprang through plashy
weed,
O'er slippery ridges, to the rock whereon
She lay with upturned face and close-shut eyes—
One hand across her breast, the other dipped
Within a shallow pool of emerald water,
With blue-veined fingers clutching the red fronds
Of frail sea-weed. Then Oswald, bending, felt
Upon his cheek the feeble breath that still

Fluttered between the pallid, parted lips.
In trembling haste, he loosed the sodden cords
That bound her to a spar ; and with hot hands
He chafed her icy limbs, until the glow
Of life returned. With fitful quivering
The white lids opened ; and she looked on him
With dull, unwondering eyes, whose deep-sea blue
The gloom of death's late passing shadowed yet;
When suddenly light thrilled them, and bright
    fear
Flashed from their depths, and, with a little gasp,
She strove to rise ; but Oswald with quick words
Calmed her weak terror, and she sank once more,
Closing her eyes ; and, gently lifting her
Within his arms—her gold hair hanging straight
And heavy with sea-water, as he plunged
Knee-deep through pools of crackling bladder-
    weed—
He bore her, unresisting, o'er the isle
Unto the rock-built shelter he had reared,
Some little way apart from his own cell,
For storm-stayed fishers or wrecked mariners.
He laid her on a bed of withered bents,
And ministered to her with gentle hands

And ceaseless care ; till, wrapped in warm, deep
    sleep,
She sank oblivious.   Silently he placed
His island-fare beside her on the board,
Lest she should wake in need ; then, with
    hushed step,
He turned to go ; but, ere he reached the door,
He paused, and looked again towards the bed,
As though he feared his strange sea-guest might
    flee
Like some wild spirit, born of wondering foam,
That wins from man the shelter of his breast,
Then, on a night of moon-enchanted tides,
Leaps with shrill laughter to its native seas,
Bearing his soul within its glistening arms,
To drown his peace on earth and hope of heaven
In cold eternities of lightless deeps.
But still in dreamless sleep the stranger lay,
With parted lips and breathing soft and calm ;
About her head unloosed, her hair outshone,
Among the grey-green bents, like fine, red gold.
So beautiful she was that Oswald, pierced
With quivering rapture, dared no longer bide,
But, with quick fingers, softly raised the latch,

And stumbled o'er the threshold. As he went,
A flock of sea-gulls from the bent-thatched roof
Rose, querulous, and round him, wheeling, swept,
With creaking wings and cold, black eyes
    agleam ;
Yet Oswald saw them not, nor heard their cries ;
Nor saw he, as he paced the eastern crags,
How, round the Farnes, the dreaming ocean lay
In broad, unshadowed, sapphire ecstasy,
That glowed to noon through slow, uncounted
    hours.
His early gloom had vanished ; time and space
And earth and sea no longer compassed him ;
One thought alone consumed him—beauty slept
Within the shelter of his hermitage,
Upon grey, rustling bents, with golden hair.
He roamed, unresting, till the copper sun
Sank in a steel-grey sea, and earth and sky
Were strewn with shadows—wavering and dim—
To weave a pathway for the dawning moon,
That she, from night's oblivion, might create
With the cold spell of her enchantments old
A phantom earth with magical, bright seas,
A vaster heaven of unrevealèd stars.

Unmoving, on a headland of swart crag
That jutted gaunt and sharp against the night,
Stood Oswald, cowled and silent. Hour by hour
He gazed across the sea, which nothing
    shadowed,
Save where—now dim, now white—a lonely sail
Hung, restless, o'er a fisher's barren toil.
Yet Oswald saw nor sail nor moon nor sea:
His heart kept vigil by the little house
Wherein the stranger slumbered; and it seemed
His life, by some strange power within him stayed,
Awaited the unlatching of the door.

But now, within the hut, the sleeper dreamt
Of foaming caverns and o'erwhelming waters;
Then, shuddering awake, awhile she lay,
And watched the moonlight, cold and white, which poured
    which poured
Through the warm dusk, from the high window-
    slit;
When, all at once, the strangeness of the room
Closed in upon her with bewildering dread.
She stirred; the bents, beneath her, rustled
    strange;

She started in affright, and, swaying, stood
Within the streaming moonlight, till, at last,
In memory, once more disaster swept
Over her life, and left her, desolate,
Upon bleak crags of alien seas unknown.
Yet, through the tumult of tempestuous dark,
Above the echo of despairing cries,
A calm voice sounded ; and beyond the whirl
Of foaming death, wherein she caught the gleam
Of well-loved faces drowning in cold seas,
A living face shone out—a beacon clear :
Then numbing fear fell from her, and she moved,
Unlatched the door, and stole into the night.
One moment, dazzled by the full-moon glare,
She paused, a shivering form within the wide
And glittering desolation—lone and frail.
But Oswald, watchful on the eastern scars,
Seeing her, forward came with eager pace
To meet her ; and, as he drew swiftly near,
His cowl fell backward ; and she knew again
The face that calmed the terrors of her dreams.
Yet, with the knowledge, through her being stole,
Vague fear more strange, more impotent than
    the blind

Unquestioning dread when death had round
  her stormed ;
No peril of the body could arouse
Such ecstasy of terror in her soul,
Which seemed upborne upon the shivering crest
Of some great wave, just curving, ere it crash
Upon the crags of time.   Yet, though she feared
When Oswald paused, uncertain, quick she spake,
As though she sought to parry doom with words.
She questioned him—scarce heeding his replies—
How she had hither come ; when, suddenly,
Sped by her fluttering words, the last, dim cloud
Rolled from her memory, and she saw revealed
Within a pitiless glare of naked light
The utmost horror of her desolation.
Mute with despair, she stood with parted lips,
And then cried fiercely : " Hath the sea upcast
None other on this shore ?   Am I, alone,
Of all my kin who sailed in that doomed ship,
Flung back to life ? " And as, with piteous glance,
He answered her : " Ah God, that I, with them,
Had died !   O traitor cords that held too sure
My body to the broken spar of life !
O feeble seas, that fumed in such wild wrath,

Yet could not quench so frail a thing as I ! "
With passionate step, across the isle she ran,
And leapt from crag to crag, until she stood
Upon a dizzy scar that jutted sheer
Above low-lapping waves.   Then once again
Her moaning cry was heard among the Isles :
" O bitter waters, give them back to me !
You shall not keep them ; all your waves of woe
Cannot withhold from me those dauntless lives
That were my life.   Surely they cannot rest
Without me; even from your unfathomed graves
Surely my love will draw them to my arms ! "
As though in tremulous expectation tranced,
She yearned, with arms outstretched ; as dawn
        arose
Exultant from the sea, and with clear rays
Kindled her wind-tost hair to streaming flame.

Awhile she stood, then, moaning, slowly sank
Upon the crag ; and Oswald came to her
With words of comfort which unloosed her pent
And aching woe in swift, tumultuous tears.
Oswald, in silent anguish, drew apart,
Gazing, unseeing, o'er the dawning waves ;

Until at last the tempest of her grief,
In low and fitful sobbing, spent itself;
When, turning to him, once again she spake,
And, shuddering, with faltering voice, outpoured
The tale of her despair: and Oswald heard
How she, who sat thus strangely by his side,
Marna, a sea-earl's daughter, had besought
Her father, when the old sea-hunger lit
His eyes—as waves shot through with stormy
    light—
For leave to bear him company but once,
When, with his sons, he rode the adventurous
    seas;
How he had yielded with reluctant love;
And how, from out the firth of some far strand,
Their galley rode, beneath a flaming dawn;
How her young heart had leapt to see the sails
Unfurled to take the wind, as, one by one,
Toil-glistening rowers shipped the dripping oars,
And loosened every sheet before the breeze;
How, as the ship with timbers all astrain,
Leapt to mid-sea, through Marna's body thrilled
A kindred rapture, and there came to her
The sheer, delirious joy of them true-born

To wander with the foam—each creaking cord
That tugged the quivering mast unto her singing
Of unknown shores and far, enchanted lands,
Beyond the blue horizon; how, all day,
They rode,undaunted, through the spinning surf;
But, as the sun dipped, in the cold, grey tide,
The wind, that since the dawn with steady speed
Had filled the sails, now came in fitful gusts,
Fierce and yet fiercer, till the sullen waves
Were lashed to anger, and the waters leapt
To tussle with the furies of the air ;
And how the ship, in the encounter caught,
Was tossed on crests of swirling dark, or dropped
Between o'er-toppling walls of whelming night ;
How in those hours—too dread for thought or
        speech—
Her father's hand had bound her to a spar ;
And, even as—the cord between his teeth—
He tugged the last knot sure, the vessel crashed
Upon a cleaving scar ; and she but saw
The strong, pale faces looking upon death,
Before the fierce, exultant waters closed
With cold oblivion o'er them ; and no more
She knew, until she waked within the hut,

To find her world, in one disastrous night,
In one swift surge of roaring darkness, swept
From her young feet; her kindred, home and
    friends,
And all familiar hopes and joys and fears
Dropt like a garment from her life, which now
Stood naked on the edge of some new world
Of unknown terrors.
                Oswald heard her tale
With pitying glance; yet in his eyes arose
A strange, new light, which as each gust of grief
Shook out the fluttering words, more brightly
    burned;
So that, when Marna ceased, it seemed to her
That he, in holy contemplation rapt,
Had heeded not her woe; and from her heart
Burst out a cry: " Ah God, I am alone! "
But, stung by her shrill anguish, Oswald waked
From his bright reverie, and his shining eyes
Darkened with swift compassion, as he turned
And, trembling, spake: " Nay, not alone . . ."
    Then mute
He stood—his pale lips clenched—as though
    within

There surged a torrent which he dared not loose.
Marna looked wondering up ; but, when her eyes
Saw the white passion of his face, her soul
Was tossed once more on crests of unknown
    fears ;
Yet rapture warred with terror in her heart ;
She trembled, and her breath came short and
    quick.
She dared not raise her eyes again to his,
Till, on her straining ears, his words, once more,
Fell, slow and cold and clear as water dripping
Between locked sluice-gates : " Nothing need
    you fear.
Beyond the sea of unknown terrors lie
White havens of an undiscovered peace.
For even this bleak, scar-embattled coast
May yield safe harbour to the storm-spent soul.
Your world has fallen from you that you may
Enter another world, more beautiful,
Built 'neath the shadow of the throne of God.
There shall you find new friends, who yet will
    seem
Familiar to your eyes, because their souls
Have passed through kindred perils and despairs."

He ceased ; and silence, trembling, 'twixt them
    hung ;
Till Marna, gazing yet across the sea,
Rent it with words : " Where may I find this
    peace ? "
And Oswald answered : " In an inland dale
The Sisters of the Cross await your coming,
With ever-open gate.   Within seven days,
My brethren from the mainland will put out,
Bringing me food ; on their return with them
You may embark.   Till then, this barren rock
Must be your home."   Exultant light once more
Leapt, flashing, in the depths of his dark eyes.
Yet Marna looked not up, but, slowly, spake :
" Yea, I must go. . . . But you. . . ."
    Then in dismay
She stopped, as though the thought had slipped
    unknown
From her full heart ; but Oswald caught the
    words,
And spake with hard, quick speech, as if to
    baffle
Some doubt that strove within him : " On this
    Isle

I bide, till God shall kindle my weak soul
To burn, a beacon o'er His lonely seas."
Once more he paused; and perilous silence
    swayed
Between them, until Oswald, quaking, rose,
As one who dared no longer rest beneath
O'er-toppling doom.   Yet, with calm voice, he
    spake:
" Even within this wilderness abides
Such beauty that, in your brief sojourn here,
Your soul shall starve not; all about you sweeps
The ever-changing wonder of the sea ;
But if, too full of bitter memories,
The bright waves darken, you may lift your
    eyes
To watch the swooping gull ; the flashing tern ;
The stately cormorant and the kittiwake—
Most beautiful of all the island-birds ;
Or, if your woman's heart should crave some
    grace
More exquisite, see, frail bell-campions blow,
As foam-flowers on the shallow, sandy turf."
As thus he spake, a light in Marna's eyes
Arose, and sorrow left her for awhile:

And she with bright glance questioned him, and
  watched
The hovering gulls, and plucked the snowy
  blooms,
With little cries at each discovered beauty.
Yet Oswald by her side walked silently,
And watched, as one struck mute with anguished
  fear,
Her eager eyes, and heard her chattering words.
Then, suddenly, he left her, but returned
Within the hour, with faltering step, and spake
With tremulous voice: "We two must part
  awhile;
For I must keep lone vigil in my cell
Six days and nights, with fasting and with
  prayer;
Meanwhile, within the little hut for you
Are food and shelter till the brethren come,
When I must give you over to their care."
Marna, with wondering heart, looked up at him;
But such a wild light flickered in his eyes
She dared not speak; and, shuddering, he
  turned,
And strode back swiftly to the hermitage.

Marna looked after him with yearning gaze,
As though her heart would have her call him
    back,
Yet her lips moved not; motionless, she watched
Until he passed from sight; then, sinking low
Among the flowers, she wept, she knew not why.

And, as the door closed on him, Oswald fell
Prone on the cold, black, vigil-furrowed rock
That paved his narrow cell; and long he lay
As in the clutch of some dread waking-trance,
Nor stirred until the shadows into night
Were woven.   Then unto his feet he leapt
With this wild cry: " O God, why hast Thou sent
This scourge most bitter for my naked soul ?
I feared not storm nor solitude, O God ;
I shrank not from the tempest of Thy wrath ;
Though oft my weak soul wavered, trampled o'er
By deedless hours, and yearned unto the world,
Ever afresh Thy love hath bound me fast
Unto this island of Thy lonely seas ;
And I, who deemed that I at last might reach—
I who had come through all—Thy golden haven,
Knew not Thy hand withheld this last despair,

This scourge most bitter, being most beautiful."
Then on his knees he sank, and tried to pray
Before the Virgin's shrine, where ever burned
His votive taper with unfailing light.
But when his lips would breathe the holy name,
His heart cried: "Marna! Marna!" Every pulse
Throbbed " Marna !" And his body shook and
    swayed,
As though it strove to utter that one word,
And cry it once unto eternal stars,
Though it should perish crying. Through the cell
The silence murmured: "Marna!" And without
A lone gull wailed it to the windy night.
He lifted his wild eyes, and in the shrine
He saw the face of Marna, which outburned
The flickering taper ; on the gloom up-surged,
Foam-white, the face of Marna ; till the dark
Flowed pitiful o'er him, and on the stone
He sank unconscious. Night went slowly by,
And pale dawn stole in silence through his cell ;
And, in the light of morn, the taper died,
With feeble guttering ; yet he never stirred,
Though noonday waxed and waned.
                            But Marna roamed

All night beneath the stars.   To her it seemed
That not until the closing of the door
Had all hope perished : now death tore, afresh,
Her father and her brothers from her arms.
By day and night and under sun and moon
She roamed unresting—seeing, heeding naught—
Till weariness o'ercame her, and she slept ;
And, as she slumbered, snowy-plumèd peace
Nestled within her heart ; and, when she waked,
She only yearned for that dim, cloistral calm,
Embosomed deep in some bough-sheltered vale,
Whither the boat must bear her.
                                                    In his cell,
As night paled slowly to the seventh morn,
Oswald arose—the fire within his eyes
Yet more intense, more fierce.   With eager hand
He clutched the latch, and, flinging wide the door,
He strode into the dawn.   One moment, dazed,
As though bewildered by the light, he paused ;
But, when his glance in restless roving fell
On Marna, standing on the western crag
Against the setting moon, beneath the dawn,
His passion surged upon him, and he shook ;
Then, springing madly forth, he, stumbling, ran,

And, falling at her feet upon the rock,
His voice rang out in fearful exultation:
"You shall not go! I cannot let you go!
Has not the tumult tossed you to my breast?
Yea, and not all the storms of all the seas
Shall drag you from me! Nay, you shall not go!
For we will live together on this isle
Which time has builded in the deeps for us—
We two together, one in ecstasy,
Throughout eternity; for time shall fall
From off us; and the world shall be no more:
And God, if God should stand between us
  now . . ."
Faltering, he paused; and Marna stood, afraid,
Quaking before him; but she spake no word.
Across the waters came the plash of oars;
But Oswald heard them not, and once more
  cried:
" You will not go—thrusting me back to death?
For now I know the strange, new thing you
  brought
For me from out the storm was life—yea, life;
And I am one arisen from the grave.
You will not thrust me back and take again

That which you came through storm to bring to
  me?
You will not go? I cannot let you go!"

He ceased; and now the even plash of oars
Came clearer. One dread moment Marna stood
Swaying; then, stretching forth her arms, she
  cried:
"Ah God! Ah God! Why hath Thy cold hand
  set
This doom upon me? Must I ever bear
Death and disaster unto whom I love?
Oh, is it not enough that, 'neath the wave,
Because I sought to bear them company,
My father and my brothers lie in death?
But this—ah God—that it should come to this!
Must I bear ever death within my hands?"

She paused one moment, with wild-heaving
  breast;
Then, turning unto Oswald, spake again,
With softer voice: "But you—have you no pity?
You who are but God's servant—surely you
Have pity on my weakness. From this doom

Which overhangs me you must set me free.
You say I brought you life ; but in me lies
For you—the priest of God—a death more deep
Than all the drowning fathoms of the sea.
I go, that you may live.   If life indeed
I brought you, I was but the torch of God
To kindle the clear flame of your strong soul
To burn, a beacon o'er His lonely seas."
She ceased, with arms outstretched and lighted
        eyes.
As on some holy vision Oswald gazed
In rapt, adoring fear ; nor spake, nor stirred.
Near, and yet nearer, drew the plash of oars ;
And, turning in the boat, the brethren looked
With wondering eyes upon them, whispering :
        " Lo,
Some seraph-messenger of God most high
Tarries with Oswald. See the strange new peace
That burns his face like a white altar-flame.
Not yet must we draw near, lest our weak sight
Be blinded by that glory of gold hair
That gleams so strangely in the light of dawn."

The Unknown Knight

WHEN purple gloomed the wintry ridge
　　Against the sunset's windy flame,
From pine-browed hills, along the bridge,
　　An unknown rider came.

I watched him idly from the tower.
　　Though he nor looked nor raised his head;
I felt my life before him cower
　　In dumb, foreboding dread.

I saw him to the portal win
　　Unchallenged, and no lackey stirred
To take his bridle when within
　　He strode without a word.

Through all the house he passed unstayed,
　　Until he reached my father's door;
The hinge shrieked out like one afraid;
　　Then silence fell once more.

All night I hear the chafing ice
  Float, griding, down the swollen stream ;
I lie fast-held in terror's vice,
  Nor dare to think or dream.

I only know the unknown knight
  Keeps vigil by my father's bed :
Oh, who shall wake to see the light
  Flame all the east with red ?

The King's Death

The sleeping-chamber of the King : a candle burns dimly by the curtained bed. The arras parts, and two slaves enter with daggers. A storm of wind rages without.

FIRST SLAVE : He sleeps.

SECOND SLAVE : He sleeps, whom only death
    shall rouse
To dread unsleeping in another world.

FIRST SLAVE : How long the careful night has
    kept him wakeful,
As if sleep loathed to snare him for our knives !

SECOND SLAVE : Yea, we have crouched so
    close in quaking dark
I scarce can lift my sword-arm : strike you first.

FIRST SLAVE : The heavy waiting hours have
    crushed my strength ;
The hate that burst to such an eager flame
Within my heart has smouldered to dull ash,

Which pity breathes to scatter.

   SECOND SLAVE : Knows he pity ?

   FIRST SLAVE : Nay, he is throned above his
    slaughtered kin,

A reeking sword his sceptre. He has broken,

As one across the knee a faggot snaps,

Strong lives to feed the blaze of his ambition ;

Yet shall a slave's hand strike cold death in him

For whom kings sweat like slaves ?

   SECOND SLAVE : Yea, at the stroke

One slave lies dead—a hundred kings are born ;

For every man that breathes will be a king ;

Vast empires, beaten-dust beneath his feet,

Will rise again and teem with kingly men,

When he, their death, is dead

   FIRST SLAVE : How still he sleeps !

The tempest shrieks to wake him, yet he
    slumbers.

As seas that foam against unyielding scars,

The mad wind storms the castle, wall and tower,

And is not spent. Hark, it has found a breach—

Some latch unloosed—the house is full of wind ;

It rushes, wailing, down the corridor ;

It seeks the King ; it cries on him to waken ;

Now 'tis without, and shakes the rattling bolt;
Lo, it has broken in, in little gusts,
I feel it in my hair; 'twill lay cold fingers
Upon his lips, and start him from his sleep.
See, it has whipt the yellow flame to smoke.
SECOND SLAVE: And now it fails; the heavy,
    hanging gold
That shelters him from night is all unstirred.
  FIRST SLAVE: Even the wind must pause.
  SECOND SLAVE: 'Twas but a breeze
To blow our sinking courage to clear fire.
Too long we loiter; soon the approaching day
Will take us, slaves who grasp the arms of men
Yet dare not plunge them save in our own breasts.
Come, let us strike!
(*They approach the bed and draw aside the curtain.*)
  FIRST SLAVE: The King—how still he sleeps!
Can majesty in such calm slumber lie?
  SECOND SLAVE: Come, falter not, strike home!
  FIRST SLAVE: Hold, hold your hand,
For death has stolen a march upon our hate;
He does not breathe.
  SECOND SLAVE: The stars have wrought for us,
And we are conquerors with unbloodied hands.

FIRST SLAVE: Nay, nay, for in our thoughts his
    life was spilt ;
While yet our bodies lagged in fettered fear,
Our shafted breath sped on and stabbed his sleep.
Oh, red for all the world, across our brows,
Our murderous thoughts have burned the brand
    of Cain.
See, through the window stares the pitiless day !

The Knight of the Wood

" I FEAR the Knight of the Wood," she said:
　　" For him may no man overthrow.
Where boughs are matted thick o'erhead,
There gleams, amid the shadows dread,
The terror of his armour red ;
And all men fear him, high and low ;
Yet all must through the forest go."

She paused awhile where larches flame
About the borders of the wood ;
Then, crying loud on Love's high name
To keep her maiden-heart from shame,
She entered, and full-swiftly came
Where, hooded with a scarlet hood,
A rider in her pathway stood.

She saw the gleam of armour red ;
She saw the fiery pennon wave

Its flaming terror overhead
'Mid writhing boughs and shadows dread.
" Ah God," she cried : " that I were dead,
And laid for ever in my grave ! "
Then, swooning, called on Love to save.

Among the springing fern she fell,
And very nigh to death she lay ;
Till, like the fading of a spell
At ringing of the matin-bell,
The darkness left her ; by a well
She waked beneath the open day,
And rose to go upon her way ;

When, once again, the ruddy light
Of arms she saw, and turned to flee ;
But clutching brambles stayed her flight ;
While, marvelling, she saw the Knight
Unhooded ; and his eyes were bright
With April colours of the sea ;
And crownèd as a King was he.

She knelt before him in the ferns,
And sang : " O Lord of Love, I bow

D

Before thy shield, where blazoned burns
The flaming heart with light that turns
The night to day.   O heart that yearns
For love, lo, Love before thee now—
The wild-wood knight with crownèd brow!"

Notre Dame de la Belle - Verrière

ABOVE Thy halo's burning blue
    For ever hovers the White Dove ;
Thy heart enshrines, for ever new,
The Cross—the Crown of all Thy love ;
While, sapphire wing on sapphire wing,
About Thee choiring angels swing
Gold censers, and bright candles bear.
Because I have no heart to sing,
I come to Thee with all my care,
Notre Dame de la Belle-Verrière.

Because the sword hath pierced Thy side,
Thy brows are crowned with circling gold.
The woe of all the world doth hide
Within Thy mantle's azure fold.
Because Thou, too, hast dwelt with fears,
Through lingering days and endless years,

I find no comfort otherwhere,
Our Lady beautiful with tears,
Our Lady sorrowfully fair,
Notre Dame de la Belle-Verrière.

My feet have travelled the hot road
Between the poppies' barren fires;
But now I cast aside the load
Of burning hopes and wild desires
That ever fierce and fiercer grew.
Thy peace falls like a falling dew
Upon me as I kneel in prayer,
Because Thou hast known sorrow, too,
Because Thou, too, hast known despair,
Notre Dame de la Belle-Verrière.

In the Valley

LOVE, take my hand, and look not with sad
    eyes
Through the valley-shades: for us, the mountains
    rise;
Beneath the cold, blue-cleaving peaks of snow
Like flame the April-blossomed almonds blow—
Spring-grace and winter-glory intertwined
Within the glittering web that colour weaves.

Yet who are they who troop so close behind
With raiment rustling like frost-withered leaves
That burden winter-winds with ever-restless sighs?

Love, look not back, nor ever hearken more
To murmuring shades; for us, the river-shore
Is lit with dew-hung daffodils that gleam
On either side the tawny, foaming stream
That bears through April with triumphal song
Dissolving winter to the brimming sea.

Yet who are they who, ever-whispering, throng,
With lean, grey lips that shudder piteously,
As if from some bright fruit of bitter-tasting core ?

Nay, look not back, for, lo, in trancèd light
Love stays awhile his world-encircling flight
To wait our coming from the valley-ways;
See where, a hovering fire amid the blaze,
He pants aflame with irised plumes unfurled
Above the utmost pinnacle of noon.

Yet who are they who wander through the world
Like weary clouds about a wintry moon,
With wan, bewildered brows that bear eternal night ?

Love, look not back, nor fill thy heart with woe
Of old, sad loves that perished long ago;
For ever after living lovers tread
Pale, yearning ghosts of all earth's lovers dead.
A little while with life we lead the train
Ere we, too, follow, cold, some breathing love.

I fear their fevered eyes and hands that strain
To snatch our joy that flutters bright above,
To shadow with grey death its ruddy, pulsing glow.

Love, look not back in this life-crowning hour
When all our love breaks into perfect flower
Beneath the kindling heights of frozen time.
Come, Love, that we with happy haste may climb
Beyond the valley, and may chance to see
Some unknown peak that cleaves unfading skies.

Old sorrow saps my strength ; I may not flee
The flame of passionate hunger in their eyes ;
Beseeching shade on shade—they hold me in their power.

Love, look not back, for, all too brief, our day,
In wilder glories flameth fast away.
Lo, even now, the northern snow-ridge glows—
With purple shadowed—from pale gold to rose
That shivers white beneath stars dawning cold.
Lift up thine eyes ere all the colour fades.

Ah, rainbow-plumèd Love in airs of gold,
Too late I turn, a shade among the shades,
To follow, death-enthralled, thy flight through ages
    grey.

The Vision.

A Christmas Mystery.

PERSONS: A Young Herd. His Mother.
SCENE: The Queen's Crags.
TIME: Christmas Eve.

The herd stands at the foot of the Crags, gazing across the dark fells. His mother enters.

MOTHER: Son, come home, nor tarry here
In this peril-haunted place.
My old heart is filled with fear
By the white flame of thy face,
And thine eyes whose restless fire
Burneth ever wild and clear
As red peats between the bars.
Son, come home; the night is cold;
Dropping from the wintry stars,
Tingling frost falls through the air;
See, the bents are white with rime;
All the sheep are in the fold;
All the cattle in the byre;
Only we, of live things, roam

O'er the fells so far from home;
E'en the red fox in his lair
Snuggles close to keep him warm;
And the lonely, wandering hare
Crouches, shivering, in her form;
While by Greenlea's frozen edge
Hides the mallard in the sedge.
Son, come home; the ingle-seat
Waits thee by the glowing peat,
And the door is off the latch.
Come, and we will feast and sing,
As of old at Christmas time,
Until thou wilt drowse and nod
And with slumber-drooping head
Gladly seek thy bracken-bed
Underneath the heather-thatch;
Where the healing sleep will bring
Unto thee the peace of God.
Son, come home! Whom seekest thou there?

HERD: Guenevere! O Guenevere!

MOTHER: Cry no more on Guenevere.
Some wild warlock of the fells,
Born beneath the Devil's Scars,

Lures thee forth to drown thy soul
Deep in Broomlea-water cold.
Guenevere no longer dwells
Anywhere beneath the stars ;
Though she walked these Crags of old,
Many hundred years ago,
Into earth she sank like snow ;
As a sunset-cloud in rain
Breaks, and showers the thirsty plain,
All the glory of her hair
Fell to earth, we know not where.
Leave thy foolish quest forlorn.
Lo, to-night a King is born,
Who, when earthly kings at last
Into wildering night are passed,
Yet shall wear the crown of morn.

Mary, Thou whose love may turn
Eyes that after evil burn,
Draw his soul, that strays so far,
To Thy Son's white throning-star.
Queen of Heaven, hear my prayer !

    HERD: Guenevere ! O Guenevere !
    MOTHER: Low she lies, and may not **hear.**

The white lily, Guenevere,
Ruthless time has trodden down;
Arthur is a tarnished crown,
High Gawain a broken spear,
Percival a riven shield;
They, who taught the world to yield,
Closed with death and lost the field,
Stricken by the last despair :
Launcelot is but a name
Blown about the winds of shame;
Surely God has quenched the flame
That burned men's souls for Guenevere.

Mary, heed a mother's woe ;
Mary, heed a mother's tears !
Thou, whose heart so long ago
Knew the pangs and hopes and fears
We poor mortal mothers know ;
Thou, to whom, on Christmas-morn,
Christ, the Son of God, was born ;
Thou whose mother-love hath pressed
The sweet Babe against thy breast ;
And with wondering joy hath felt
The warm clutch of little hands,

When the Kings from far-off lands—
Crowned with gold, in gold attire—
With the simple shepherds knelt
'Mid the beasts within the byre;
Mary, if Thy heart, afraid,
When beyond Thy care he strayed,
Sometimes grieved that he must grow
Unlike other boys and men—
Filled with dreams beyond Thy ken,
Anguished with diviner woe,
Pangs more fiery than Thy pain,
Deeper than Thy dark despair—
From the perils of the night
Give me back my son again.
Thou, whose love may never fail,
Heed a lonely mother's prayer!
Come in all Thy healing might!

A sudden glory sweeps across the Fells. The vision appears in a cleft of the Crags. The herd and his mother kneel before it.

MOTHER: Mary, Queen of Heaven, hail!

HERD (*falling forward*): Guenevere! O
        Guenevere!

THE THREE KINGS.

To C. J. S.

The Three Kings

PERSONS: KING GARLAND, KING ARLO, KING ASHALORN.

SEA-VOICES, WAVE-VOICES, AND WIND-VOICES.

SCENE: *A rock in the midst of the North Sea, whereon the three kings, bound naked by conquering sea-rovers, have been left to perish.*

VOICE OF THE DAWN-WIND: Awaken, O sea,
    from thy starry dream;
Awaken, awaken!
For delight of thy slumber not one pale gleam
From dim star-clusters remaineth unshaken.
All night I have haunted the valleys and rivers;
Now hither I come—
Ere, quickened with sunlight, the drowsy east
    quivers—
To waken thy song, night-bewildered and dumb;
To stir thy grey waters, of starlight forsaken,
To loosen white foam in the red of the dawn.

WAVE-VOICES: The sound of thy voice
Has broken our sleep;
All night we have waited thee, herald of light.
We arise, we rejoice
At thy bidding to leap,
And spray with our laughter the trail of the night.
All night we have waited thee, weary of stars—
The little star-dreams, and the sleep without song;
The deep-brooding slumber of silence that holds
Our melody mute in the uttermost deep.
O Wind of the Dawn, we have waited thee long;
The sound of thy voice
Has broken our sleep;
We arise, we rejoice
At thy bidding to leap,
With a tumult of singing, a rapture of spray,
To scatter our joy in the path of the day.

GARLAND: Day comes at last, beyond the
    sea's grey rim;
The young sun leaps in sudden might of gold.

ASHALORN: Before his fire our lives will
    smoulder dim;
Like stars we shine, we fade; the tale is told,

And all our empty splendour put to scorn;
Fate leaves us, who were clothed in pride, forlorn,
To perish, naked, in this lonely sea.
But yesterday we ruled as kings of earth;
Frail men to-day; to-morrow, who shall be?

ARLO: But yesterday my cup of life was filled
To overflowing with the wine of mirth—
The plashing joy from fruitful years distilled.

GARLAND: But yesterday my kinghood sprang
    to birth;
My fingers scarce had grasped the might new-
    born,
When from my clutch the glittering pomp was
    torn.

SEA-VOICES: They slumber, they slumber,
    the kings in their pride.
The beak of the Rover is dipt in the tide;
The sails of the Rover are red in the wind;
And white is the trail of the foam flung behind.

They have fallen, have fallen, the kings in their
    pride;

E

Their sea-gates are forced by the rush of the tide;
Their splendour is scattered as surf on the wind ;
And red is the trail of the terror behind.

Forsaken, forlorn,
On a rock of the sea,
In anguish they bow,
And wait for the night and the darkness to be ;
Oh, bright was the gold in their hair ;
The sea-weed, in scorn,
Is twined in it now ;
Oh, rich was their raiment and rare,
Blue, purple, and gold,
In fold upon fold ;
Of glory and majesty shorn,
They are clothed with the wind of despair.

    GARLAND : Lo, the live waters run to greet
      the day :
Even so I laughed to see the soaring light ;
My life was poised like yonder curving wave
To break in such bright revel of keen spray.

    ARLO : I counted not the years that took their
      flight,

Gold-crowned and singing; every hour I stood,
As one enchanted in an April wood,
In some new paradise of scent and flowers.
I counted not the countless, careless hours,
The days of rapture and the nights of peace.
How should I dream that such delight could pass,
Such colour fade, such flowing numbers cease,
My glory perish where was none to save,
And all my strength be trodden in the grass?

ASHALORN: Oh, blest art thou who diest in
    thy youth;
Oh, blest art thou who failest in thy prime;
While yet thine eyes are full of wondering truth;
Ere yet thy feet have found the ways of thorn.
Too long I wandered down the vale of time,
A lonely wind, all songless and forlorn;
For I have found the empty heart of things,
The secret sorrow of the summer rose,
And all the sadness of the April green;
I know that every happy stream that springs
Into a sea of bitter memories flows;
I know the curse that God has set on kings—
The solitary splendour and the crown

Of desolation, and the prisoning state;
The heart that yearns beneath the robe of gold,
The soul that starves behind the golden gate.
I know how chance has reared our earthly
      thrones
Upon a shifting wrack of whitened bones,
Of heroes fallen in the wars of old—
By wind upbuilded and by wind cast down.

   SEA-VOICES: As foam on the edge of the waters
      of night,
They flicker and fall;
More brief than delight,
More frail than their tears,
They flicker and fall
In the tide of the years;
Awhile they may triumph, as lords of the earth,
With feasting and mirth,
Yet the winds and the waters shall sweep over all.

   VOICE OF THE WEST WIND: O wide-shifting
      wonder of sapphire and gold,
O wandering glory of emerald and white,
From the purple and green of the moorlands I
      come,

To sweep o'er thy waters with turbulent flight,
To sway thee, and swing thee abroad in my
    might :
I lean to thy lips, to their white, curling foam,
With laughter and kisses, to smite it to spray ;
To thine uttermost deep, unlitten and cold,
I thrill thee with rapture, then wander away.

I have drunk the red wine of the heather, and
    swept
Over moorland and fell, for mile upon mile.
The little blue loughs were merry, and leapt,
With a shaking of laughter, in dim, dreaming
    hollows ;
The little blue loughs were merry, and flung
Their spray on my wings as above them I swung;
I laughed to their laughter, and dallied awhile ;
Then left them to sink in the silence that follows.

In the forest I stirred, like the chant of thy tides,
The song of the boughs and the branches
    a-swinging ;
The ashes and beeches and oak-trees were sing-
    ing,

Like the noise of thy waters when dark tempest
    rides.
I swung on the crest of the pine-trees a-swaying,
As now on thy green, flowing surges, O sea;
I piped in my triumph, they danced to my playing;
I left them a-murmur, to hasten to thee.

The white clouds were driven like ships through
    the air,
And grey flowed the shadows o'er sea-coloured
    bent,
And dark on the heathland, and dark on the wold:
But here on thy waters, where all things grow
    fair,
They shadow with purple thine emerald and
    gold.
My revel unbroken, my rapture unspent,
To thy far-shining wonder, O sea, I have come,
To sweep o'er thy splendour with turbulent
    flight;
To sway thee, and swing thee abroad in my
    might;
I lean to thy lips, to their white, curling foam,
With laughter and kisses, to smite it to spray;

To thine uttermost deep, unlitten and cold,
I thrill thee with rapture, then wander away.

GARLAND : There is no sadness in the world
    but death.
The years that whitened o'er thy head have taken
The colour from thy life, but still in me
The blood beats young and red; yea, still my
    breath
Is full of freshness as the wind that blows
Across the morning-fells when night has shaken
His cooling dews among the wakening heath.
Yea, now the wind that lashes o'er the sea
Stings all my quivering body to keen life
And whips the blood into my straining limbs;
And all the youth within me springs to fire;
I am consumed with ravening desire
For one brief, wild, delirious hour of strife;
I yearn for every joy that flies or swims,
Rides on the wind or with the water flows.
Yet I must die by patient, slow degrees,
With hourly wasting flesh and parching blood;
Ah God, that I might leap into the flood,
And perish struggling in the adventurous seas!

ARLO : My mouth is filled with saltness, and
    I thirst
For forest-pools that bubble in the shade,
When loud the hot chase pants through every
    glade,
And fleeing fawns from every thicket burst ;
Or clear wine vintaged when the world was
    young,
Gurgling from deep-mouthed jars of coloured
    stone.

ASHALORN : The noonday burns my body to
    the bone,
And sets a coal of fire upon my tongue,
Between my lips, and stifles all my breath.
Oh come, thou only joy undying, death !

WAVE-VOICES : O wind, that failing, failing,
    failing, dies,
Beneath the heat of August-laden skies,
Sinking in sleep, sinking in quiet sleep—
Thy blue wings folded o'er our dreaming deep

We too are weary, weary in the noon ;
We too will fall in shining slumber soon—

Foamless and still, foamless and very still,
Unstirred, unshaken by thy restless will.

Yet there are eyes that cannot, cannot close,
And strong souls racked by fiery, rending woes—
Never to rest, never to gather rest
By any stream of murmuring waters blest.

But slumber falling, falling, on us lies,
Silent and deep, beneath noon-laden skies,
Silent and deep, silent and very deep,
With blue wings folded o'er our dreaming sleep.

.   .   .   .   .

VOICE OF THE EVENING WIND : I have shaken
    the noon from my wings, I arise
To quicken the flame in the western skies—
To blow the clouds to a streaming flame,
Where the red sun sinks in the opal sea,
And red as the heart of the opal glows
His last wild gleam in the waters grey.
O grey-green waters, curling to rose,
The kings are glad of the dying day ;
The kings are weary ; the white mists close—
The white mists gather to cover their shame.

ASHALORN : The evening mist is dank upon
    my brow,
And cold upon my lips—yea, cold as death;
Yet, through the gloom, she gazes on me now,
As in our early-wedded days; her breath
Is warm once more upon my withered cheek.
O gaunt, grey lips, that strive but may not
    speak;
O cold, grey eyes, that flicker in the gloam—
Long have we strayed; come, let us wander
    home!

ARLO : Like lit September woodlands, stream-
    eth down
Her hair, beneath the circle of her crown;
Of rarer, redder glory than the cold
Dead metal that for ever strives to hold
The ever-straying wonder of live gold!
Like woodland pools, her eyes, a dreaming
    brown—
Like woodland pools where autumn-splendours
    drown!
O red-gold tresses, shaking in the gloam,
Unto your light, unto your shade I come!

GARLAND: Her eyes are azure as the wind-
    blown sea,
With deep sea-shadowings of grey and green;
And like an April storm her shining hair—
Yea, all the glittering Aprils that have been,
And all the wondering Aprils yet to be,
Have stored their wealth of shower and sunshine
    there;
Yea, all the thousand, thousand springs of earth
New-lit and re-awakened at her birth,
In her sweet body glow and glimmer fair.
O wonder of sea-colours and white foam
And April glories, to thine arms I come!

VOICE OF THE EVENING WIND: The sun is
    gone, and the last, red flame
Has faded away in a shimmer of rose—
A shimmer of rose that shivers to grey.
The kings are glad of the dying day—
The kings are weary; the white mists close,
The white mists gather to cover their shame.

THE SONGS OF QUEEN AVERLAINE.

To M. B.

PERSONS: THE KING,

QUEEN AVERLAINE,

THE KNIGHT ARKELD.

I.

KING AND QUEEN.

I.

THE day has come; at last my dream unfolds
  White, wondering petals with the rising
    sun.
No other glade in Love's world-garden holds
  So fair a bloom from vanquished winter won.

Long, oh, so long I watched through budding
    hours,
  And, trembling, feared my dream would never
    wake;
As, one by one, I saw star-trancèd flowers
  Out on the night their dewy splendour shake.

But with the earliest gleam of dawn it stirred,
  Knowing that Love had put the dark to flight;
And I must sing more glad than any bird
  Because the sun has filled my dream with light.

2.

IS it high noon, already, in the land?
    O Love, I dreamed that morn could never
        pass;
That we might ever wander, hand in hand,
As children in June-meadows plucking flowers, ˙
Through ever-waking, fresh-unfolding hours:
Yet now we sink love-wearied in the grass;
Yea, it is noon, high noon in all the land.

The young wind slumbers; all the little birds
That sang about us in the fields of morn
Are songless now; no happy flight of words
On Love's lip hovers—Love has waxed to noon.
Ah, God, if Love should wane to evening soon
To perish in a sunless world, forlorn,
And cease with the last song of weary birds!

3.

AT dawn I gathered flowers of white,
To garland them for your delight.

At noon I gathered flowers of blue,
To weave them into joy for you.

At eve I gather purple flowers,
To strew above the withered hours.

4.

SHE knelt at eve beside the stream,
　　And, sighing, sang: " O waters clear,
Forsaken now of joy and fear,
I come to drown a withered dream.

" Unseen of day, I let it fall
Within the shadow of my hair.
O little dream, that bloomed so fair,
The waters hide you after all! "

5.

" IS it not dawn?" she cried, and raised her
head,
" Or hath the sun, grey-shrouded, yesternight,
Gone down with Love for ever to the dead?
When Love has perished, can there yet be light?"

" Yea, it is dawn," one answered : " see the dew
Quivers agleam, and all the east is white ;
While in the willow song begins anew."
" When Love has perished, can there yet be
light?"

II.

AVERLAINE AND ARKELD.

I.

ARKELD : Oh, why did you lift your eyes to
mine ?
Oh, why did you lift your drooping head ?

AVERLAINE : The tangled threads of the fates
entwine
Our hearts that follow as children led.

ARKELD : From the utmost ends of the earth
we came,
As star moves starward through wildering night.

AVERLAINE : Our souls have mingled as flame
with flame,
Yea, they have mingled as light with light.

ARKELD : Ah God, ah God, that it never had
been !

AVERLAINE : The Shadow, the Shadow that
falls between !

ARKELD : The stars in their courses move
   through the sky
Unswerving, unheeding, cold and blind.

AVERLAINE : Why did you linger nor pass me
   by
Where the cross-roads meet in the ways that
   wind ?

ARKELD : I saw your eyes from the dusk of
   your hair
Flame out with sorrow and yearning love.

AVERLAINE : And I, who wandered with grey
   despair,
Looking up, saw heaven in blossom above.

ARKELD : Ah God, ah God, that it never had
   been !

AVERLAINE : The Shadow, the Shadow that
   falls between !

ARKELD : May we not go as we came, alone,
Unto the ends of the earth anew ?

AVERLAINE: May we draw afresh from the
rose new-blown
The golden sunlight, the crystal dew?

ARKELD: Yea, love between us has bloomed
as a rose
Out of the desert under our feet.

AVERLAINE: May we forget how the red heart
glows,
Forget that the dew on the petals is sweet?

ARKELD: Ah God, ah God, that it never had
been!

AVERLAINE: The Shadow, the Shadow that
falls between!

ARKELD: Have the ages brought us together
that we
Might tremble, start at shadows, and cry?

AVERLAINE: Yea, it has been, and ever will be
Till Sorrow be slain or Love's self die.

ARKELD: Stronger than Sorrow is Love; and Hate,
The brother of Love, shall end our Sorrow.

AVERLAINE: The Shadow is strong with the strength of Fate,
And, slain, would rise from the grave to-morrow.

ARKELD: Ah God, ah God, that it never had been!

AVERLAINE: The Shadow, the Shadow for ever between!

2.

AVERLAINE: Yea, we must part, and tear with
  ruthless hands
The golden web wherein, too late, Love strove
To weave us joy and bind us heart to heart.

ARKELD: Yea, we must part, and strew on
  desert-sands
Petal by petal all the rose of Love,
And part for ever where the cross-ways part.

AVERLAINE: Yea, we must part, and never
  turn our eyes
From strange horizons, desolate and far,
Though Love cry ever: "Turn but once, sad
  heart!"

ARKELD: Yea, we must part, and under alien
  skies
Must follow after some cold, gleaming star,
And roam, as north and south winds roam, apart.

AVERLAINE: Yea, we must part, ere Love be
   grown too strong
And we too helpless to resist his might ;
While each may go with pure, unshamèd heart.

ARKELD: Yea, we must part ; and though we
   do Love wrong,
He will the more subdue us in our flight,
And hold us each more surely his, apart.

III.

QUEEN AVERLAINE.

I.

O LOVE, I bade you go; and you have borne
The summer with you from the valley-lands;
The poppy-flame has perished from the corn;
And in the chill, wan light of early morn
The reapers come in doleful, starveling bands,
To bind the blackened sheaves with listless
    hands;
For rain has put their sowing-toil to scorn.

O Love, I bade you go; and autumn brings
Bleak desolation; yet within my heart
Unquenched and fierce the flame you kindled
    springs;
For, echoing all day long, the courtyard rings
As loud it rang when, rending Love apart,
Your white horse cantered—swift and keen to
    start—
Into a world of other queens and kings.

2.

I BADE you go ; ah, wherefore are you gone?
  How could you leave me dark and desolate,
O Sun of Love, that for brief summer shone?
Mine eyes are ever on the western gate,
Half-wishing, half-foredreading your return.
Return, O Love, return!

I cannot live without you ; through the dark
I stretch blind hands to you across the world ;
All day on unknown battle-fields I mark
Your sword's red course, your banner blue
    unfurled ;
Yet never, in my day-dreams, you return.
Return, O Love, return!

Nay, you are gone: O Love, I bade you go.
I would not have you come again to be
A stranger in this house of silent woe,
Where, being all, you would be naught to me.
Mine, mine in dreams, but lost if you return ;
Oh, nevermore return!

3.

TO-DAY a wandering harper came
   With outland tales of deeds of fame;
I hearkened from the noonday bright
Until the failing of the light,
The while he sang of joust and fight;
Yet never once I caught your name.

Oh, whither, whither are you gone,
Whose name victorious ever shone
Above all knights of other lands?
Across what wilderness of sands?
By what dead sea-deserted strands?
On what far quest of Love forlorn?

I loved you when men called you Lord
Arkeld, the never-sleeping sword;
Yet now, when all your might is furled,
And you no longer crest the world,
More are you mine than when you hurled
Destruction on the embattled horde.

G—2

QUEEN AVERLAINE

4.

OH, deeper in the silent house
  The silence falls ;
Only the stir of bat or mouse
  About the walls.

No cry, no voice in any room,
  No gust of breath ;
As if, within the clutch of doom,
  We waited death.

5.

THE King is dead;
    No longer now
The cold eyes gleam
    Beneath his brow.

O cold, grey eyes,
    Wherein the light
Of Love at dawn
    Seemed clear and bright,

No true Love burned
    Your cold desire,
Which mirrored but
    My own heart's fire.

6.

THE King died yesterday. . . . Ah, no,
   he died
When young Love perished long, so long ago;
And on his throne, as marble at my side,
   Has reigned a carven image, cold as snow,
Though all men bowed before it, crying: "King!"

Too late, too late the chains which held me fall;
   Rock-bound, I bade the victor-knight go by;
And now, when time has loosed me from the thrall,
   I know not where he tarries, 'neath what sky
He waits the winter's end, the dawn of spring.

7.

SPRING comes no more for me: though
    young March blow
To flame the larches, and from tree to tree
The green fire leap, till all the woodlands glow—
Though every runnel, filled to overflow,
Bear sea-ward, loud and brown with melted snow,
Spring comes no more for me!

Spring comes no more for me: though April light
The flame of gorse above the peacock sea;
Though in an interweaving mesh of white
The seagulls hover 'neath the cliff's sheer height;
Though, hour by hour, new joys are winged for
    flight,
Spring comes no more for me!

Spring comes no more for me: though May will
    shake
White flame of hawthorn over all the lea,
Till every thick-set hedge and tangled brake
Puts on fresh flower of beauty for her sake;
Though all the world from winter-sleep awake,
Spring comes no more for me!

8.

I WANDERED through the city till I came
   Within the vast cathedral, cool and dim;
I looked upon the windows all aflame
   With blazoned knights and saints and seraphim.

I looked on kings in purple, gold and blue,
   On martyrs high before whom all men bow;
Until a gleam of light my footsteps drew
   Before a shining seraph, on whose brow

A little flame, for ever pure and white,
   Unwavering burns—the symbol of our love;
And as I knelt before him in the night,
   He looked, compassionate, on me from above.

9.

I HEARD a harper 'neath the castle walls
  Sing, for night-shelter in the house of thralls,
A song of hapless lovers; in the shade
I paused awhile, unseen of man or maid.

Taking his harp, he touched the moaning strings,
And sang of queens unloved and loveless kings;
His song shot through my fluttering heart like
    flame
Till, wondering, I heard him breathe your name.

Oh, then I knew how all the deathless wrong
Time wrought of old is but a harper's song;
And all the hopeless sorrow of long years
An idle tale to win a stranger's tears.

Yea, in the song of Love's immortal dead
Our love was told; with shuddering heart I fled,
And strove to pass upon my way unseen,
But song was hushed with whispers: " Lo, the
    Queen ! "

10.

WAS it for this we loved, O Time, to be
  Among Love's deathless through eternity,
Set high on lone, divided peaks above
The sheltered summer-valley, broad and green?
Was it for this our joy and grief have been,
Our barren day-dreams, dream-deserted nights—
That valley-lovers, looking up, might see
How vain is Love among the starry heights,
And, loving, sigh: "How vain a thing is Love!"?

O Love, that we had found thee in the shade
Where, all day long, the deep, leaf-hidden glade
Hears but the moan of some forsaken dove,
Or the clear song of happy, nameless streams;
Where, all night long, the August moonlight
  gleams
Through warm, green dusk, no longer cold and
  white!
O Love, that we had found thee, unafraid,
One summer morn, and followed thee till night,
As unknown valley-lovers follow Love!

II.

I HAVE grown old, awaiting spring's return,
   And, now spring comes, I stand like winter
      grey
In a young world; yet warm within me burn
   The morning-fires Love kindled in youth's day.

I have grown old; the young folk look on me
   With sighs, and wonder that I once was fair,
And whisper one another: "Is this she?
   Did summer ever light that winter hair?

"Ah, she is old; yet, she, too, once was young:
   Yea, loved as we love even, for men tell
How bright her beauty burned on every tongue,
   And how a knightly stranger loved her well.

"Yet Love grows old that beats so young and
      warm;
   His leaping fires in dust and ashes fail;
Shall we, too, wither in the winter-storm,
   And wander thus one April, old and frail?"

Love grows not old, O lovers, though youth die,
  And bodily beauty perish as the flower ;
Though all things fail, though spring and
    summer fly,
  Love's fire burns quenchless till the last dark
    hour.

12.

O VALLEY-LOVERS, think you love,
    Being all of joy, knows naught of sorrow?
A day, a night
Of swift delight
That fears no dread, grey-dawning morrow ?

O valley-lovers, think you love
Knows only laughter, naught of weeping ?
A rose-red fire
Of warm desire
For ever burning, never sleeping ?

O lovers, little know ye Love.
Love is a flame that feeds on sorrow—
A lone star bright
Through endless night
That waits a never-dawning morrow.

13.

THUS would I sing of life,
    Ere I must yield my breath:
Though broken in the strife,
I sought not after death.
Though ruthless years have scourged
My soul with sorrow's brands,
And, day by day, have urged
My feet o'er desert-sands;
Yet would I rather tread
Again the bitter trail,
Than lie, calm-browed and pale,
Among the loveless dead.

No pang would I forego,
No stab of suffering,
No agony of woe,
If I to life might cling;
If I might follow still,
For evermore, afar,

O'er barren dale and hill,
My Love's unfading star.
Yea, now, with failing breath,
Thus would I sing of life:
Though broken in the strife,
I sought not after death.

14.

DARKNESS has come upon me in the end;
    Darkness has come upon me like a friend,
Yet undesired; why comest thou, O night,
To seal mine eyes for ever from the light?

Darkness has come upon me; yet a star
Burns through the night and beckons me from far.
Look up, O eyes, unfaltering, without fear;
O morning-star of Love, the dawn is near!

THE GOLDEN HELM.

H

The Golden Helm

A CROSS his stripling shoulders Geoffrey felt
   The knighting-sword fall lightly, and he
    heard
The King's voice bid him rise ; and at the word
He rose, new-flushed with knighthood, swiftly
   grown
To sudden manhood, though, but now, he knelt
A vigil-wearied squire before the throne.
He paused one moment while the people turned
To look on him with eyes that kindled bright,
Seeing his face aglow with strange, new light ;
Yet them he saw not where they watched amazed,
And, though like azure flames Queen Hild's
   eyes burned,
Beyond the shadow of the throne he gazed
To where, in kindred rapture, young Christine
Stood, tremulous and white, in wind-flower
   grace—
Beneath her thick, dark hair, her happy face

Pale-gleaming 'midst the ruddy maiden-throng;
But, following Geoffrey's eyes, the trembling
    Queen
Now bade the harpers rouse the air with song:
From pulsing throat and silver-throbbing string
The music soared, light-winged, and, fluttering,
    fell;
When, startled as one waking from a spell,
Geoffrey stepped back among the waiting
    knights;
While knelt another squire before the King.
In Queen Hild's eyes yet hovered stormy lights,
Beneath her glooming brows, as waters gleam
Under snow-laden skies; the summer day
For her in that brief glance had shivered grey,
Empty of light and song. She only heard
The King and knights as people of a dream;
Yet keenly Geoffrey's lightest, laughing word
Stung to the quick, and stabbed her quivering
    life,
Till from each shuddering wound the red joy
    flowed;
And, though a ruddy fire on each cheek glowed,
She felt her drainèd heart within her cold;

Then all at once a hot thought stirred new
    strife
Within her breast, and suddenly grown old
And wise in treacherous imagining,
She pressed her thin lips to a bitter smile,
And strove with laughing mask to hide the guile
That, slowly welling, through her body poured
Cold-blooded life that feels no arrowy sting
Of joy or hope, nor thrust of pity's sword.
To Christine, where she yet enraptured stood,
Hild, turning, spake kind words, and coldly
    praised
The new-made knight. Each word Christine
    amazed
Drank in with joyous heart and eager ears;
To her it seemed ne'er lived a Queen so good;
And love's swift rapture filled her eyes with tears.
For her true heart, the day-long pageant moved
Round Geoffrey's shining presence; king and
    knight
But shone for her with pale, reflected light.
As trancèd planets circling round the sun,
About the radiant head of her beloved
The dim throngs moved until the day was done.

When lucent gold suffused the cloudless west,
And lingering thrush-notes failed in drowsy song,
She left, at last, the weary maiden-throng,
To stray alone through dew-hung garden-glades;
And all the love unsealed within her breast
Flowed out from her to light the darkest shades.
Her quivering maiden-body could not hold
The suddén welling of love's loosened flood;
Through all her limbs it gushed, and in her blood
It stormed each throbbing pulse with blissful ache;
It seemed to spray the utmost glooms with gold,
And scatter glistening dews in every brake.
While yet she moved in rapture unafraid
Among the lilies, down the Grey Nun's Walk,
She heard behind the snapping of a stalk,
And stayed transfixed, nor dared to turn her head,
But stood a solitary, trembling maid—
Forlorn and frail, with all her courage fled.
Thus Geoffrey found her as, hot-foot, he pressed
To pour about her all the glowing tide
Day-pent within his heart; the flood-gates wide,
His love swept over her, sea after sea,
Until life almost swooned within her breast,
And she seemed like to drown in ecstasy.

Yet, as the tempest sank in calm at last,
She rose from out the foam of love, new-born—
As Venus from the irised surf of morn—
To such triumphant beauty, Geoffrey, thralled,
Before her stood in wonder rooted fast;
Even his love within him bowed appalled
In tongueless worship as he gazed on her;
While, lily-like, the trancèd flowers among,
She stood, love-radiant, and above her hung
The canopy of star-enkindling night;
Though, when again she moved with joyous stir,
He sprang to her in love's unchallenged might.

II.

All night, beside her slumbering lord, the Queen
Tossed sleepless—every aching sense astrain
With tingling wakefulness that racked like pain
Her weary limbs; all night, in wide-eyed dread,
She watched the slow hours moving dark between
The glimmering window and the curtained bed.
The fitful calling of the owl, all night,
Struck like the voice of terror on her ears;
With brushing wings, about her taloned fears

Fluttered till dawn : when, as the summer gloom,
Grey-quivering, spilt in silver-showering light;
She rose and stood within the dawning room,
Shivering and pale—her long, unbraided hair
Each moment quickening to a livelier gold
About her snowy shoulders; yet, more cold
Than the still gleam of winter-frozen meres,
Her blue eyes shone with strange, unseeing stare,
As though they sought to pierce some mist of
    fears ;
And, when she turned, the old familiar things
Unknown and alien seemèd to her sight—
Outworn and faded in the morning light
The rose-embroidered tapestries, and frail
The painted Love that hung on irised wings
Above the sleeping King. Dark-browed and pale
She looked upon her lord, and fresh despair
With dreadful calm through all her being stole,
And froze with icy breath the flickering soul
That strove within her.   Evil courage steeled
Her heart once more, as, combing back her hair,
She watched the waking world of wood and field :
Hay-harvesters with long scythes flashing white;
The dewy-browsing deer ; the blue smoke-curl

Above some woodland hut ; a kerchiefed girl
Driving the kine afield with loitering pace.
But, as a youthful rider came in sight,
She from the casement turned with darkening
     face,
And looked not out again, and fiercely pressed
Her white teeth in her quivering underlip,
To stifle the wild cry that strove to slip
From her strained throat ; with clutching hands
     she sought
To stay the throbbing tumult of her breast
That fluttered like a bird in meshes caught.

Christine as yet in dreamless slumber lay
Within her turret-chamber ; but a bird
Within the laurel singing softly stirred
Her eyes to wakeful life, and from her bed
She rose and stood within the light of day,
White-faced and wondering, with lifted head.
As April-butterflies, new-winged for flight,
That poise awhile in quivering amaze,
Ere they may dare the unknown, glittering ways
Of perilous airs—upon the brink of morn
She paused one moment in the showering light,

In radiant ecstasy of youth forlorn.
Then swift remembrance flushed her virgin snow,
And wakened in her eyes the living fire ;
With joyous haste she drew her bright attire
About her trembling limbs, with eager hands,
Veiling her maiden beauty's morning glow,
Before she looked abroad on meadowlands,
Where Geoffrey rode at dawn. Across the blaze
Of dandelions silvering to seed,
She saw his white horse swing with easy speed ;
He rode with head exultant in the breeze
That lifted his brown hair. With lingering gaze
She watched him vanish down an aisle of
    trees ;
Then, swiftly gathering her dark hair in braids
Above her slender neck, she crossed the floor
With noiseless step, unlatched the creaking door,
And stole in trembling silence down the stair,
Intent to reach the garden ere the maids
Should come with chattering tongues and
    laughter there ;
When by her side she heard a rustling stir :
The arras parted, and before her stood
Queen Hild in proud, imperious womanhood,

Looking upon her with cold, smiling eyes.
In startled wonder Christine glanced at her.
Then spake the Queen: " Do maids thus early
  rise
To tend their household duties, or to feed
The doves, relinquishing sleep's precious hours
To see the morning dew upon the flowers
And what frail blooms have perished 'neath the
  moon?
To reach the Grey Nun's Walk, mayhap you
  speed—
To count the stricken buds of lilies strewn
O'ernight upon the soil by careless feet
That wandered there so late? Yea, now I know,
Christine, because you flush and tremble so.
Yet look you not on me with eyes that burn;
I would not stay you when you go to greet
The rider of the dawn on his return.
Think you I leave my bed at break of day—
I, Hild the Queen—to thwart a lover's kiss?
Think you my love of you could stoop to this,
Though you would wed a fledgling, deedless
  Knight?
Nay, shrink you not from me, turn not away;

Because my heart has never known love's light,
I fain would hear your happy tale of love,
That I may prosper you and your fair youth.
Will you not trust me?" Blind with love's
glad truth,
Christine sank down within Hild's outstretched
arms.
Speechless, awhile, with sobbing breath she
strove;
Then poured out all the tale of love's alarms,
Raptures, despairs, and deathless ecstasies,
In one quick torrent from her brimming heart;
Then, quaking, ceased, and drew herself apart,
Dismayed that she so easily had revealed
To this white, cold-eyed Queen love's sanctities.
Yet Hild moved not, but stood, with hard lips
sealed,
Until, the chiming of the turret-bell
Recalling her, she spake with far-off voice:
" I, loveless, in your innocent love rejoice.
May nothing stem its eager raptured course!
Oh, that my barren heart could love so well,
And feel the surge of love's subduing force!
Yet even I from out my dearth may give

To you, Christine.   Would you that Geoffrey's
      name
Shall shine, unchallenged, on the lists of fame ?
If you would have him win for you the crown
Of knightly immortality, and live
Triumphant on men's tongues in high renown,
Follow me now."   With cold, exulting eyes
She raised the arras, opening to the light
An unknown stair-way clambering into night.
Within the caverned wall she swiftly passed.
Christine for one brief moment in surprise
Uncertain paused; then, wondering, followed
      fast.
The falling arras shutting out the day,
She stumbled blindly through the soaring
      gloom—
Enclosing dank and chilly as the tomb
Her panting life ; and unto her it seemed
That ever, as she climbed, more sheer the way
Before her rose, and ever fainter gleamed
The wan, white star of light that overhead
Hovered remote.   Far up the stair she heard
A silken rustling as, without a word,
Relentlessly Queen Hild before her sped

For ever up the ever-soaring steep.
But when it almost seemed that she must fall—
So loudly in her ears the pulses beat,
And each step seemed to sink beneath her feet—
She heard the shrilly grating of a key,
And saw, above her, in the unseen wall,
A dazzling square of day break suddenly.
Within the lighted doorway Queen Hild turned
To reach a helping hand, and, as she bent
To clutch the swooning maiden, well-nigh spent,
And drew her to the chamber, weak and faint,
Through her gold hair so rare a lustre burned,
It seemed to Christine that an aureoled saint
Leaned out from heaven to snatch her from the
        deep.
Then, dizzily, she sank upon the floor,
Dreaming that toil was over evermore,
And she secure in Love's celestial fold;
Till, waking gradually as from a sleep,
Her dark eyes opened on a blaze of gold.
She sat within a chamber hung around
With glistering tapestry, whereon a knight,
Who bore a golden helm above the fight,
For ever triumphed o'er assailing swords,

Or led the greenwood chase with horse and
    hound,
While far behind him lagged the dames and lords
And all the hunting train ; till he, at length,
Brought low the antlered quarry on the brink
Of some deep, craggy cleft, wherefrom did shrink
The quailing hounds with lathered flanks aquake.
As Christine looked on them, her maiden-strength
Returned to her ; and now, more broad awake,
She saw, within the centre of the room,
A golden table whereon glittered bright
A casket of wrought gold, and, in the light,
Queen Hild, awaiting her, with smiling lips,
And laughing words : " Is this then love's sad
    doom,
To perish, fainting, in light's brief eclipse
Between a curtain and a closèd door ?
Shall this bright casket ever hold, unsought,
The golden helm—in elfin-ages wrought
For some star-destined knight—because love's
    heart
Grows faint within her ? Shall the world no more
Acclaim its helmèd lord ? " But, with a start,
Christine arose, and swiftly forward came

With eager eyes, and stooped with fluttering
    breast—
Her slender, shapely hands together pressed
In tense expectancy, and all her face
With quivering light of wondering love aflame.
The Queen bent down, and in a breathing space
Unlocked the casket with a golden key,
And deftly loosed a little golden pin;
The heavy lid swung open and, within,
To Christine's eyes revealed the golden helm.
Then spake Queen Hild, once more : " Your
    love-gift see!
Think you that any smith in all the realm
Can beat dull metal to so fair a casque ?
In jewelled caverns of enchantment old
This helm was wrought of magic-tempered gold
To yieldless strength, by elfin-hammers chased,
That toiled unwearied at their age-long task,
And over it an unknown legend traced
In letters of some world-forgotten tongue.
At noon, with careful footing, down the stair
Unto the hall the casket you must bear,
When King and knight are gathered round the
    board,

And, ere the tales be told or songs be sung,
Acclaim your love the golden-helmèd lord."
Christine, awhile, in speechless wonderment,
Hung o'er the glistering helm, and silence fell
Within the arrased chamber like a spell;
While softly, on some distant, sunlit roof,
The basking pigeons cooed with deep content;
Till, far below, a sudden-clanging hoof
Startled the morn.   The women's lifted eyes
One moment met in kindred ecstasy;
Then Hild, with hopeless shudder, shaking free,
With strained voice spake : " Why do you
        longer wait ?
Your love returns; shall he, in sad surprise,
Find no glad face to greet him at the gate ? "

III.

As some new jest was tossed from tongue to
        tongue,
Light laughter rippled round the midday board,
Beneath the bannered rafters : dame and lord
And maid and squire with merry chattering
Sat feasting; though no motley humour wrung

A smile from Hild, where she, beside the King,
Watched pale and still.   She saw on Geoffrey's
    face
Grave wonder that he caught not anywhere
Among the maids the dusk of Christine's hair,
Or sunlight of her glance.   His eyes, between
The curtained doorway and her empty place,
Kept eager, anxious vigil for Christine.
But when, at last, the lingering meal nigh o'er,
The waking harp-notes trembled through the
    hush,
Like the light, fitful prelude of the thrush
Ere his full song enchant the domèd elm ;
The arras parting, through the open door
She came.   Before her borne, the golden helm
Within the dim-lit hall shone out so bright,
That lord and dame in rustling wonder rose,
And squire and maiden sought to gather close,
With questioning lips, about the love-bright
    maid.
Christine, unheeding, turned nor left nor right ;
With lifted head and eager step unstayed,
She strode to Geoffrey, while he stood alone,
Radiant with wondering love—as one who sees

The light of high, eternal mysteries
Illume awhile the mortal shade that moves
From out oblivion unto night unknown,
Hugging a little grace of joys and loves.
Before him now she came and, kneeling, spake,
With slow, clear-welling voice : " In ages old
This helm was wrought from elfin-hammered
    gold,
For one who, in the after-days, should be
Supreme above his kind, as, in the brake
Of branching fern, the solitary tree
That crests the fell-top.   Unto you I bring
The gift of destiny, that, as the sun
New-risen of your knighthood, newly-won,
The wondering world may see its glory shine."
As Christine spake, with questioning glance the
    King
Turned to the Queen, who gave no answering
    sign.
Then, stretching forth his arm, he cried : "Sir
    knight,
I know not by what evil chance this maid
Has climbed the secret newell-stair unstayed
And reached the casket-chamber, and has borne

From thence the Helm of Strife, whereon the
    light
Of day has never fallen, night or morn,
For seven hundred years ; but, ere you take
The doomful gift, know this : he who shall dare
To don the golden helm must ever fare
Upon the edge of peril, ever ride
Between dark-ambushed dangers, ever wake
Unto the thunderous crash of battle-tide.
Oh, pause before you take the fateful helm.
Will you, so young, forego, for evermore,
The sheltered haven-raptures of the shore,
To strive in ceaseless tempest, till, at last,
The fury-crested wave shall overwhelm
Your broken life on death's dark crag upcast ? "
He ceased, and stood with eyes of hot appeal ;
An aching silence shuddered through the hall ;
None stirred nor spake, though, swaying like to
    fall,
Christine, in mute, imploring agony,
Wavered nigh death. As glittering points of steel
Queen Hild's eyes gleamed in bitter victory.
But all were turned to Geoffrey, where he stood
In pillared might of manhood, very fair ;

His face a little paled beneath his hair,
Though bright his eyes with all the light of
    day.
At length he spake : " For evil or for good,
I take the Helm of Strife ; let come what may."

IV.

Dawn shivered coldly through the meadowlands ;
The ever-trembling aspens by the stream
Quivered with chilly light and fitful gleam ;
Ruffling the heavy foliage of the plane,
Until the leaves turned, like pale, lifted hands,
A cold gust stirred with presage of near rain.
Coldly the light on Geoffrey's hauberk fell ;
But yet more cold on Christine's heart there lay
The winter-clutch of grief, as, far away,
She saw him ride, and in the stirrup rise
And, turning, wave to her a last farewell.
Beyond the ridge he vanished, and her eyes
Caught the far flashing of the helm of gold
One moment as it glanced with mocking light ;
Then naught but tossing pine-trees filled her
    sight.

Yet darker gloomed the woodlands 'neath the
    drench
Of pillared showers ; colder and yet more cold
Her heart had shuddered since the last, hot
    wrench
Of parting overnight. Though still her mouth
Felt the mute 'mpress of love's sacred seal ;
Though still through all her senses seemed to
    steal
The heavy fume of wound-wort that had hung·
All night about the hedgerows—parched with
    drouth ;
Though the first notes the missel-cock had sung,
Ere darkness fled, resounded in her ears ;
Yet no hot tempest of tumultuous woe
Shook her young body. As night-fallen snow
Burdens with numb despair young April's green,
Her sorrow lay upon her ; hopes and fears
Within her slept. As something vaguely seen
Nor realised—since yesterday's dread noon
Had shattered all love's triumph—life had passed
About her like a dream by doom o'ercast.
Long hours she sat, with silent, folded hands,
And face that glimmered like a winter moon

In cloudy hair.   Across the rain-grey lands
She gazed with eyes unseeing ; till she heard
A step within her chamber, and her name
Fell dully on her ear ; then like a flame
Sharp anguish shot through every aching limb
With keen remembrance.   Suddenly she stirred,
And, turning, looked on Hild.   " Grieve you for
      him . . ."
The Queen began ; then, with a little gasp,
Her voice failed, and she shrank before the gaze
Of Christine's eyes, and, shrivelled by the blaze
Of fires her hand had kindled, all her pride
Fell shredded, and not even the gold clasp
Of queenhood held, her naked deed to hide.
She quailed, and, turning, fled from out the
      room.
Soon Christine's wrath was drowned in whelm-
      ing grief,
And in the fall of tears she found relief—
As brooding skies in sweet release of rain.
All day she wept, until, at length, the gloom
Of eve laid soothing hands upon her pain.
Then, once again, she rose, calm-browed, and
      sped

Downstairs with silent step, and reached, un-
    stayed,
The Grey Nun's Walk, where all alone a maid
Drank in the rain-cooled air. With low-breathed
    words,
They whispered long together, while, o'erhead,
From rain-wet branches rang the song of birds.
The maiden often paused as in alarm;
Then, with uncertain, half-delaying pace,
She left Christine, returning in a space
With Philip, Christine's brother, a young squire,
Who strode by her with careless, swinging arm
And eager face, with keen, blue eyes afire.
Then all three stood, with whispering heads
    bent low,
In eager converse clustered; till, at last,
They parted, and, with high hopes beating fast,
Christine unto her turret-room returned—
Her dark eyes bright and all her face aglow,
As if some new-lit rapture in her burned.
About her little chamber swift she moved,
Until, at length, in travelling array,
She paused to rest, and all-impatient lay
Upon her snow-white bed, and watched the light

Fail from the lilied arras that she loved
Because her hand had wrought each petal white
And slender, emerald stem. The falling night·
Was lit for her with many a memory
Of little things she could no longer see,
That had been with her in old, happy hours,
Before her girlish joys had taken flight
As morning dews from noon-unfolding flowers.
For her, with laggard pace the minutes trailed,
Till night seemed to eternity outdrawn.
At last, an hour before the summer-dawn,
She rose and once again, with noiseless tread,
Crept down the stair, grey-cloaked and closely
    veiled,
While every shadow struck her cold with dread
Lest, drawing back the arras, Hild should stand
With mocking smile before her ; but, unstayed,
She reached the stair-foot, and, no more afraid,
She sought a low and shadow-hidden door,
Slid back the silent bolts with eager hand,
And stepped into the garden dim once more.
She quickly crossed a dewy-plashing lawn,
And, passing through a little wicket-gate,
She reached the road. Not long had she to wait

Ere, with two bridled horses, Philip came.
Silent they mounted; far they fared ere dawn
Burnished the castle-weathercock to flame.

V.

Northward they climbed from out the valley mist;
Northward they crossed the sun-enchanted fells;
Northward they plunged down deep, fern-hidden
    dells;
And northward yet—until the sapphire noon
Had burned and glowed to thunderous amethyst
Of evening skies about an opal moon;
Northward they followed fast the loud-tongued
    fame
Of young Sir Geoffrey of the golden helm;
Until it seemed that storm must overwhelm
Their weary flight. They sought a lodging-place,
And soon upon a lonely cell they came
Wherein a hermit laboured after grace.
On beds of withered bracken, soft and warm,
He housed them, and himself, all night, alone,
Knelt in long vigil on the aching stone,
Within his little chapel, though, all night,

His prayers were drowned by thunders of the
    storm,
And all about him flashed blue, pulsing light.
Christine in calm, undreaming slumber lay,
Nor stirred till, clear and glittering, the morn
Sang through the forest; though, with roots
    uptorn,
The mightiest-limbed and highest-soaring oak
Had fallen charred, with green leaves shrivelled
    grey.
At tinkling of the matin-bell she woke,
And soon with Philip left the woodland boughs
For barer uplands.   Over tawny bent
And purpling heath they rode till day was spent;
When, down within a broad, green-dusking dale,
They sought the shelter of the holy house
Of God's White Sisters of the Virgin's Veil.
So, day by day, they ever northward pressed,
Until they left the lands of peace behind,
And rode among the border-hills, where blind
Insatiate warfare ever rages fierce;
Where night-winds ever fan a fiery crest,
And dawn's light breaks on bright, embattled
    spears:

A land whose barren hills are helmed with towers;
A lone, grey land of battle-wasted shires;
A land of blackened barns and empty byres;
A land of rock-bound holds and robber-hordes,
Of slumberous noons and wakeful midnight hours,
Of ambushed dark and moonlight flashing
    swords.
With hand on hilt and ever-kindling eyes,
Flushed face and quivering nostril, Philip rode;
But nought assailed them; every lone abode
Forsaken seemed; all empty lay the land
Beneath the empty sky; only the cries
Of plovers pierced the blue on either hand
Until, at sudden cresting of a hill,
The clang of battle sounded on their ears,
And, far below, they saw a surge of spears
Crash on unyielding ranks; while, from the sea'
Of striving steel, with deathly singing shrill, .
A spray of arrows flickered fitfully.
Amazed they stood, wide-eyed, with holden
    breath;
When, of a sudden, flashed upon their sight
The golden helm in midmost of the fight,
Where, with high-lifted head and undismayed,

Sir Geoffrey rode, a very lord of death,
With ever-leaping, ever-crashing blade.
Christine watched long, now cold with quaking
    dread,
Now hot with hope as each assailant fell;
The bright sword held her gaze as by a spell;
Because love blinded her to all but love,
Unmoved she watched the foemen shudder dead,
She whose heart erst the meanest woe could
    move.
Then, dazed, she saw a solitary shaft,
Unloosed with certain aim from out the bow,
Strike clean through Geoffrey's hauberk, and
    bring low
The golden helm, while o'er him swiftly met
The tides of fight.   Christine a little laughed
With rattling throat, and stood with still eyes
    set.
Scarce Philip dared to raise his eyes to hers
To see the terror there.   No word she spake,
But leaned a little forward through the brake
That bloomed about her in a golden blaze;
Her hands were torn to bleeding by the furze,
Yet nothing could disturb that dreadful gaze.

Then, gradually, the heaving battle swerved
To northward, faltering broken, and afar
It closed again, where, round a jutting scar,
The flashing torrent of the river curved.
With eager step Christine ran down the hill,
And sped across the late-forsaken field
To where, with shattered sword and splintered
    shield,
Among the mounded bodies Geoffrey lay.
She loosed his helm, but deathly pale and still
His young face gleamed within the light of
    day.
Christine beside him knelt, as Philip sought
A draught of water from the peat-born stream;
When, in his eyes, at last, a fitful gleam
Flickered, and bending low, with straining ears,
The laboured breathing of her name she caught;
And over his dead face fell fast her tears.
Once more towards them the tide of battle swept;
Christine moved not. Young Philip on her cried,
And strove, in vain, to draw her safe aside.
A random shaft in her unshielded breast—
Though hot to stay its course her brother leapt—
Struck quivering, and she slowly sank to rest.

VI.

Queen Hild sat weaving in her garden-close,
When on her startled ear there fell the news
Of Christine's flight before the darkling dews
Had thrilled with dawn. A strand of golden
      thread
Slipped from her trembling fingers as she rose
And hastened to the castle with drooped head.
All morn she paced within her blinded room,
Unresting, to and fro, her white hands clenched ;
All morn within her tearless eyes, unquenched,
Blue fires of anger smouldered, yet no moan
Escaped her lips.   Without, in summer bloom,
The garden murmured with bliss-burdened drone
Of hover-flies and lily-charmèd bees ;
Sometimes a finch lit on the window-ledge,
With shrilly pipe, or, from the rose-hung hedge,
A blackbird fluted ; yet she neither heard
Nor heeded aught ; until, by rich degrees,
Drowsed into noon the noise of bee and bird.
Yea, even when, without her chamber, stayed
A doubtful step, and timid fingers knocked,
She answered not, but, swiftly striding, locked

Yet more secure, with angry-clicking key,
The bolted door, and the affrighted maid
Unto the waiting hall fled, fearfully.
Wearied at last, upon her bed Queen Hild
In fitful slumber sank ; but evil dreams
Of battle-stricken lands and blood-red streams
Swirled through her brain.   Then, suddenly, she
　· woke,
Wide-eyed, and sat upright, with body chilled,
Though in her throat the hot air seemed to choke.
Swiftly she rose ; then, binding her loosed hair,
She bathed her throbbing brows, and, cold and
　calm,
Downstairs she glided, while the evening-psalm
In maiden-voices quavered, faint and sweet,
And from the chapel-tower, through quivering
　air,
The bell's clear silver-tinkling clove the heat.
She strode into the hall where yet the King
Sat with his knights ; a weary minstrel stirred
Cool, throbbing wood-notes, throated like a bird,
From his soft-stringèd lute.   With scornful eyes
Hild looked on them and spake : " Can nothing
　sting

Your slumberous hearts from slothful peace to
    rise ?
Must only stripling-knights and maidens ride
To battle, where, unceasing, foemen wage
War on your marches, and your wardens rage
In impotent despair with desperate swords,
While you, O King, with sheathèd arms abide ?"
She paused, and, wondering, the King and lords
Looked on her mutely ; then, again, she spake :
" Shall I, then, and my maidens sally forth
With battle-brands to conquer the wild north ?
Yea, I will go !   Who follows after me ? "
As by a blow struck suddenly awake,
The King leapt up, and, like a clamorous sea,
The knights about him.   Scornfully the Queen
Looked on them : " So my woman's words have
    roused
The hands that slumbered and the hearts that
    drowsed.
Make ready then for battle ; ere seven days
Have passed, the dawn must light your armour's
    sheen,
And in the sun your pennoned lances blaze."
Her voice ceased ; and a pulsing flame of light

K

Flashed through the hall ; in crashing thunder
    broke
The heavy, hanging heat ; the rafters woke
In echo as the rainy torrent poured ;
Bright gleamed the rapid lightning ; yet more
    bright
The war-lust kindled hot in every lord.
To clang of armour the seventh morning stirred
From slumber ; restless hoof and champing bit
Aroused the garth ; and day, arising, lit
A hundred lances, as, each bolt withdrawn,
The courtyard-gate swung wide with noise far-
    heard,
And flickering pennons rode into the dawn —
Before his knights, the King, and at his side,
Queen Hild, with ever-northward-gazing eyes ;
But, ere they far had fared, in mute surprise
They stayed and all drew rein, as down the road
They saw a little band of warriors ride—
Sore travel-stained—who bore a heavy load
Upon a branch-hung litter ; while before
Came Philip, bearing a war-broken lance.
Though King and lords looked, wondering, in a
    glance

Queen Hild had read the sorrow of his face
And pierced the leaf-hid secret—which e'ermore
A brand of fire upon her heart would trace.
Darkness about her swirled, but, with a fierce
Wild, conquering shudder, shaking herself free,
Unto the light she clung, though like a sea
It surged and eddied round her; yet so still
She sat, none knew her steely eyes could pierce
The leafy screen. With guilty terror chill,
She heard the king speak—sadly riding forth:
" Whence come you, Philip, battle-stained and
    slow ?
What burden bear you with such brows of
    woe ?"
Then Philip answered, mournfully: " I bring
Two wanderers home from out the perilous north.
Prepare to gaze on death's defeat, O King."
They lowered the litter slowly to the ground;
Back fell the branches; in the light of day,
In calm, white sleep Christine and Geoffrey
    lay,
And at their feet the baleful Helm of Strife
Sword-cloven. Hushed stood all the knights
    around,

When spake the King, alighting: " Come, O wife,
And let us twain, with humble heads low-bowed,
Even at the feet of love triumphant stand,
A little while together, hand in hand."
The Queen obeyed ; but, fearfully, she shrank
Before the eyes of death, and, quaking, cowed,
With moaning cry, low in the dust she sank.

PRINTED BY R. FOLKARD AND SON,
22, DEVONSHIRE STREET, QUEEN SQUARE, BLOOMSBURY.

CPSIA information can be obtained
at www.ICGtesting.com
Printed in the USA
BVHW051244040219
539409BV00028B/1862/P